Dark 2 Light

Malinda Vogel

6-27-20 M.
will and using their free will,
May they come and go safely and
from harm. Please guide them
Please protect this family and
Dear H.
...our sins and
choices and
create a blessed family

Dark

Sad, lonely and in

pain as pearl

in oyster.

Hope and hope not.

Used.

Used up too soon.

Used

again.

Holding on

to the very air,

to the very memory

of hope,

lovingkindness and

light.

Hurt

Do I know

what is true?

Do I have

a single free

thought

in my head? Betrayed:

do I

know who

to trust? Lied to:

do I know who

the good guys

are?

Do I

know

for sure?

Why am I

here?

What is my purpose?

What can I do?

Be a truth teller.

for all to go well, according

You untouched

Are loved, or

you

touched wrongly,

hurt; are

loved.

You

will be

released. You

will be

treasured.

You will be

set free and your spirit will

rise

into the air

to become

one with the light and down to the dear, green earth

to heal yourself and others.

Hope is held

In my heart

sight unseen, fist:

a promise

of

justice.

Fight for

it.

Fight for me,

for the children,

your children,

all children,

to be

safe

their innocence

redeemed

or repaired,

their trust

restored.

Evidence of hope

held in our hearts.

You will be helped

You will be

held.

You will be

healed.

You will be

treasured

and

cherished.

"See, I will not forget you.

I have carved you in the palm

of my hand."

Isaiah 49:15

What can I do?

How can I help
you, my neighbors,
all children?
Please guide me,
guide us
through this hot
month of August,
to set all things right,
to reestablish goodness
and justice.
It approaches
as a storm
marches across the sky.
Be prepared.
Be vigilant.
Prayer works.
Small actions
add up, and
in the end,
God wins.

What are you proud of?

What can you

do?

What will you

do?

Live for others, be

a light.

Shine your light

despite

the darkness,

in defiance of

the darkness and

discover your

power, your

superpower.

You

are

amazing.

"Let light shine out of darkness."

2 Cor. 4:6

What is freedom?

What is it worth?

What is its price?

Our souls

long and thirst for it

daily. Let us

approach You

and pray

and fight

for it

as has been done throughout the ages.

Good over evil.

Light over darkness.

God over Satan.

"I broke the fangs of the unrighteous

and made him drop his prey from his teeth."

Job 29:17

Thank you

For the

dark butterflies,

bright and brown birds,

tadpoles, babies

and all manner

of delicate and vulnerable

beings.

You entrust us with

their care.

Let us fight to

protect and defend them.

Let us speak up

for those who cannot

speak for themselves.

Let us be

the people you need us

to be.

"Defend the poor and the fatherless.

Do justice to the afflicted and needy."

Psalm 82:3

Sacred geometry

Runs through the
universe.
Each whorl of fern,
each feather and crystal
runs through our DNA.
Be assured
that there is a
hope and a
promise.
Walk through this
season.
Fight for us.
Fight for the ones
that can't fight
for
themselves.
Never give up.
Never give in.
Never surrender.

For this

Fresh air, good book,

toast and honey,

green grapes in a wooden bowl,

ginseng tea,

sons and daughters,

kind friends to

grab our hands

and listen

to us,

give us hugs,

rain on the roof,

small squirrel

with a chipped ear

at the window,

new job,

hot summer,

chance at

freedom,

chance to spread

our wings and

fly, we thank you.

Mourning doves

And sparrows
in your hands,
the lost, the vulnerable
in your hands,
all mankind and the
universe
in your hands
and mine.
I will do all that I can do.
To all that I meet,
all within my reach,
my influence, I will help
for you and with you.

What are my hands to do?

What is my purpose?
At times I feel
invisible.
But you see me,
see us all,
don't you?
Thank you for
never giving up
on us.
Show me ways
to be creative
and useful.
I love you.

GODWINSCH
4-27-21 pm ky

You have the design

And the

stuff of stars

and the

universe within

you.

You are stronger

than you

know.

You are loved.

Heal and rest,

beloved of God.

You are a

light to the world.

Shine on.

"I will praise you, for I am fearfully

and wonderfully made."

Psalm 139:14

You will be found

You will be remembered

and prayed over again

and again.

What can we do for you?

We are awake now.

You will be held and treasured.

God will not be mocked.

You will be avenged and loved.

We will soon behold

the fury of God and of righteous men and women.

"Weep no more; behold, the Lion of the tribe of Judah,

the Root of David, has conquered, so that he can

open the scroll and its seven seals." Rev. 5:5

Don't you give up

Exist.

Breathe.

Do it in defiance.

Do it for me.

Do it for yourself.

Get out in the sun.

Just soak it in.

Watch the birds.

Write a song.

Write your story.

Get it out,

slowly and carefully.

Be safe.

Take it slow.

Be free.

Do it for me.

Do it for yourself.

Do it for all the others.

Live.

You are loved
You are loved
flower girl

Thank you

For the simple things:

white plates and cups,

 red squirrels and birds,

art pens, gel pens,

watercolors, Japanese brushes,

food and shelter.

Thank you for the normal days.

I can work and clean,

walk, talk, see, hear,

taste and touch.

I can read and write,

study, research what's true

for myself.

I have this mind, this sense of responsibility.

This is my life.

These are my choices.

This is my country.

These are my people.

Let me be of use.

For all these things

I am grateful.

I love you

You are one of a kind,

like each dove,

each butterfly

and fingerprint is unique.

You are sharing my heart

with the world.

It can be painful

but please

shine your light

and share your heart

and vision.

Get out in the grass

Barefoot.

Breathe out and in.

Settle down.

Listen.

Learn.

Heal, heal your heart.

Ask your questions.

Do your best.

The rest will follow.

For N.V.

Seeds were planted in self/soil:

seeds, weeds, an odd thought

dropped in by a bird.

This is my garden.

I plot my way up and down the rows

between rows, humming,

weeding thistles and Johnson grass

leaving ladybugs, butterflies and worms

to help the roots of the plants

to grow, and to breathe.

I soak up the rain.

I revel in the sun

blooms uptilted, uplifted

and let out

my riot of color, and

flower, crowned with bees:

no matter who passes by or when.

Pray

Fight.

Breathe.

Run.

Rest.

Survive.

Thrive.

Seek out the truth.

Help others.

Repeat.

Live.